DOG ON A LOG™
Pup Books
Book 1

I am not a Reading Specialist or certified educator, but I do have a lot of experience teaching my daughter with dyslexia how to read. At times, it was difficult to determine what to do and how to do it. It is my hope that the information provided within this book will make the journey a bit easier for other parents. The content provided herein is for informational purposes and does not take the place of an evaluation and teaching plan provided by a credentialed educator. Every effort has been made to ensure that the content provided here is accurate and helpful for my readers. However, this is not an exhaustive treatment of the subject. No liability is assumed for losses or damages due to the information provided. You should consult a credentialed educator for specific guidance on educating your child, yourself, or others.

DOG ON A LOG Books
Tucson, Arizona

Public Domain images from www.clker.com

ISBN: 978-1648310072

Library of Congress Control Number:2019905858

www.dogonalogbooks.com

BEFORE THE SQUIGGLE CODE (A ROADMAP TO READING)

DOG ON A LOG Pup Books
Book 1

By Pamela Brookes

Edited by Nancy Mather Ph.D.

DOG ON A LOG
Parent and Teacher Guides

General Information
on Dyslexia and
Struggling Readers

The Author's Routine
for Teaching Reading

Book 1. *Teaching a Struggling Reader: One Mom's Experience with Dyslexia*

Book 2. *How to Use Decodable Books to Teach Reading*

Available for free from many online booksellers or read at: www.dogonalogbooks.com/free

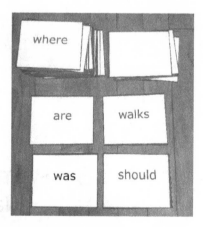

Download DOG ON A LOG printable gameboards, games, flashcards, and other activities at: www.dogonalogbooks.com/printables.

Parents and Teachers:
Receive email notifications of new books and printables. Sign up at: www.dogonalogbooks.com/subscribe

4

Table of Contents

DOG ON A LOG Parent and Teacher Guides 4

Introduction 7

The Squiggle Code 10

Adapt to Your Child 12

Words 13

THE ELK 15

PENGUINS... 21

Rhyming 27

Syllables 53

Two Words Make One(Blending Compound Words) 54

Hear the Syllables (Segmenting Compound Words) 66

Funny Syllables Make Words (Blending Two-Syllable Words) 78

Listen for the Funny Syllables (Segmenting Two-Syllable Words) 90

Longer Words(Segmenting Three-Syllable Words) 102

Take Away a Syllable (Segmenting Words) 115

Tap the Sounds 131

Beginning Sound 135

Ending Sound 157

Middle Sound 179

Blending Sounds 201

Removing Sounds (Segmenting) 213

STRUGGLING READERS 223

What If It's NOT Dyslexia 224

The Importance of Early Intervention............ 227

How You Can Help..234

DOG ON A LOG Phonics Progression 235

DOG ON A LOG Sight Word Progression 237

DOG ON A LOG Quick Assessment.......................241

Endnotes for Hyperlinks......................................243

Introduction

DOG ON A LOG Books are written for anyone learning to read with phonics. They start with basic skills then slowly add more and more reading concepts. Typical learners may advance fairly quickly through the steps. Individuals with reading disabilities such as dyslexia may need additional learning strategies and a lot more repetition. However, *DOG ON A LOG Books* are written following a systematic Orton-Gillingham based phonics sequence and are perfect for individuals with dyslexia when they have the right guidance. (They are what my daughter with dyslexia reads.)

When I first started reading about teaching phonics, I often felt overwhelmed. The things I read usually had a lot of theory that needed deciphering and lots of the activities seemed more complicated than I wanted to tackle. I wrote *DOG ON A LOG Pup Books* to try and eliminate some of those feelings for other parents. These books will guide you along the path of teaching reading. Once you understand the skills that your child needs to learn, you can then add additional activities that you and your child find fun and useful.

In this book, I give an overview of the earliest steps of learning to read in a single section called *The Squiggle Code.* Then I give very simple activities you can do with your child to practice those steps. You can also download printable activities from www.dogonalogbooks.com to supplement the activities in *Pup Books.*

The second *Pup Book* is called *The Squiggle Code (Letters Make Words.)* It is where the reader starts to learn the sounds of the letters and how to combine them into words. After that book is completed, the student is ready for *DOG ON A LOG Let's GO! Books* or *DOG ON A LOG Chapter Books.* Those companion series will slowly introduce new phonics rules and give lots of chances to practice reading. (The *Let's GO! Books* and *Chapter Books* tell the same stories. The *Let's GO! Books* have a lot less text so can be less intimidating for new readers. They work as a bridge to the longer Chapter Books. You could say, "Janelle, you read the *Let's GO! Book.* The *Chapter Book* has the same type of words and you know the story. I am sure you can read it if we take our time.")

As a parent, I know how expensive it is to raise kids. To limit the production costs of the *Pup Books,* I limit the activities I include. Not every family will want the same extra activities. Some kids may like worksheets where they have to match rhyming pictures. Other kids might hate them. Those kids may prefer making up silly words that rhyme with pictures they see or a gazillion other fun activities. You can find online ideas for activities at dogonalogbooks.com, TeachersPayTeachers.com, or Pinterest.com. (Hint: Phonological Awareness refers to our ability to hear and manipulate sounds in words. Phonemic Awareness means hearing the individual sounds, called phonemes, that we give to letters.) You can also watch videos on teaching phonological awareness at www.coxcampus.org.

However, if your child is struggling and does not progress from one step to the next even though you think they are old enough to understand the material, it could be that they have a learning disability such as dyslexia. If that is the case, I recommend seeking help from a certified learning disabilities professional.

I have developed *DOG ON A LOG Books* and materials with recommendations from my daughter's reading teacher and other professionals who specialize in phonics and learning disabilities. However, coming up with strategies that can help individual learners is beyond what *DOG ON A LOG Books* are meant to do. I provide the road map and reading materials and the people that know your children can develop the methods for using the materials. The Orton-Gillingham Approach is considered the best method for teaching children with dyslexia (and possibly most learners.) I highly recommend finding a certified Orton-Gillingham instructor.

You can learn more about dyslexia in my e-booklet *Teaching a Struggling Reader: One Mom's Experience with Dyslexia.* There is information about testing, inexpensive screening tools, and how to find the right type of specialist and how to find the information you need to help your child yourself. You can read it at www.dogonalogbooks.com/free. Excerpts from two sections are included at the end of this book.

The Squiggle Code

Spoken language is a code. The code starts with random sounds that we group together into words. Then we put several words together to make sentences. By talking and by listening to each other's words and sentences, we share ideas with other human beings.

Reading and writing are another type of code for sharing ideas. This code involves squiggles. We happen to call those squiggles letters.

We put squiggles on a piece of paper and tell a child, "Tell me what this says."

Yet those squiggles are silent. They do not make any noise. Surely children must think we are crazy that we can get sounds out of squiggles.

Children trust us so they try to make that madness happen. If they are lucky, they have patient adults that show them how the squiggles make sounds and that groups of squiggles combine to make words.

Part of the best way to help someone learn to read is to make sure they can hear the smallest sounds in words which are called phonemes. And before we can teach them the small sounds, we must make sure they can hear the big sounds.

So, the beginning of learning to read is making sure the student can hear words. That may seem silly since most people learn to talk when they are just babies. Yet if they haven't thought about what a word is, how can we expect them to turn squiggles into words?

This book will help your child, or even an adult learner, learn to hear each word in a sentence. Once they can do that, they must learn to hear syllables in each word. (Identifying syllables will also be an important skill when they are trying to read. Once they are taught the six types of syllables, it will make reading and writing a lot easier.) After they can identify the syllables in a word, it will be time to hear the individual sounds, the phonemes, in a word.

And then we tell them that each sound has a squiggle. If they put those squiggles together, they will make words. And if they can look at the squiggles someone has placed on a piece of paper or on a computer screen and they can make all those squiggles make a sound, they will have broken the squiggle code. That is when reading begins.

I know what it's like to be an overwhelmed parent who is given too much information in one big chunk. To keep this book parent-friendly (not too much information all at once,) I have put the information about Struggling Readers at the back of this book. You can read it now or at your convenience.

Adapt to Your Child

This is so important it gets an entire page and two sets of arrows. This book is a roadmap. It shows you the skills your child must learn before they can proceed on the reading path. It also gives you ideas on how to introduce the skill as well as links to where you can find more activities. It is important that you use the activities and strategies that work for YOUR child. And if you have more than one child, you may need to use completely different strategies with each. When I have used this book while teaching at our homeschool co-op, I have found that sometimes I cannot follow the book exactly. That's okay because that's how kids learn. The book shows me what skill I need to teach then I find a different way of presenting it.

Of equal importance, the activities you use must also work for you. As bored as I was by doing sound cards over and over, that technique worked for my daughter. We also did the magnetic letters and played board games that had been adapted with "special cards" that were created for her reading level. At no time did I look on Pinterest for cute holiday-themed crafts that also taught letter sounds. I am not into crafts. My daughter is, so she does those types of activities at the homeschool co-operative or with her tutors, but not me. I just cannot stand doing crafts and I would have been miserable trying to find some then actually doing them. (Although if I was told the only way my daughter would ever read was by making construction paper stars, I would have done it. Fortunately, no one has said that.)

Words

Can you hear each word?

Thump Your Elbow

Read this story to your child. Have them thump their elbow or their knee for each word they hear. If it is too much work to finish the story in one sitting, then read for as long as your child can concentrate, then take a break. Come back later and pick up from where you left off.

If you have an older child who does not want to thump their elbow, you may want to have them tap a pencil on a table.

THE ELK

This is Tup.

Tup is a dog.

This is Jan.

Jan and Tup are friends.

Tup and Jan go for a walk.

They hike up a big hill.

At the top of the hill, they see an elk.

"That is Al the elk," Jan says. "I am glad to see him."

"Hi Jan and Tup. Would you like a ride?" Al says.

Jan climbs on Al's back. "Will you take us home?" she asks the elk.

"How fast should
we go?" Al asks.

"Ruff, Ruff," Tup
says.

"Got it. We will
go real fast," Al
says.

Jan holds tight to
Al's   neck.   Jan
feels the wind in
her hair.

Tup runs so fast. He does not feel the wind.

Then they are home. Al and Tup want to play.

Al and Tup race back to the hill. Tup barks, "Ruff, ruff," all the way up the hill.

If your child needs more help, you can repeat this story over and over. You can also read simple books with single syllable words or make up your own sentences to thump. You can do this during bath time, while snuggling on the couch, or any other quiet family time. You can also download printable "hear the word" activities at www.dogonalogbooks.com

Do not progress until your child has mastered this level. A builder wouldn't put a roof on a house before the concrete foundation has hardened. It is the same with the skills your child is learning here.

Once your child can thump the single syllable words in sentences, try thumping sentences that contain words with more syllables. The story *Penguins* will help you do that.

PENGUINS

Jan and Gret are sisters.

Quin and Dave are brothers.

The four friends are biking.

They ride to see Liz and her cousin Lil.

Liz and Lil stand next to the fence by a pasture.

In the pasture is a bunch of penguins.

"Why do you have penguins in the desert?" Jan asks.

"They are going to live at a penguin center," Liz says.

"The truck broke down and the penguins were getting hot," Lil says.

"My dad told the driver that the penguins could stay here," Liz says.

"I bet that the penguins are happy it is winter in the desert," Dave says.

A penguin walks to the pasture fence. He tilts his head and looks at the kids.

All six kids tilt their heads.

The penguin laughs and waddles away.

If your child needs more help hearing and thumping words with two syllables, you can repeat this story over and over. You can also thump while you read other books or make up your own sentences to thump. You can also download "hear the word" printable activities at www.dogonalogbooks.com.

Once your child can identify individual words in sentences, it is time to listen for rhyming sounds. Do not move on to rhyming until your child can consistently thump words.

Do not progress until your child has mastered this level.

Rhyming

Words rhyme when the ending sounds of two or more words are the same or very similar. For example, house/mouse or fame/plane. Read the rhyming words on the following pages to your child. Have fun saying the words and accentuating the rhyming sounds.

Dr. Sally Shaywitz (co-director of the Yale Center for Dyslexia and Creativity, at Yale University) says the biggest indicator (of dyslexia) is the inability to appreciate rhymes. "If a child doesn't seem to 'get' the funny rhymes in a Dr. Seuss book, this may be a beginning sign of a reading disorder," she says. [1]

---

[1] *Ability to Catch Dyslexia Early May Help Stem Its Effects* by Elizabeth Norton Lasley, The Dana Foundation September, 2009.
http://dana.org/Publications/Brainwork/Details.aspx?id=43792

These words rhyme.

dog

frog

log

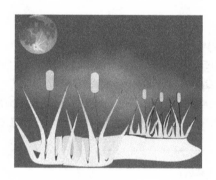

fog

28

These words rhyme.

jam

clam

lamb

ram

These words rhyme.

pink · sink

drink · mink

Are These the Same?

Now it's time to see if your child can tell which words rhyme.

Do these words rhyme?

ox fox

socks box

Do these words rhyme?

cat

bat

rat

hat

Do these words rhyme?

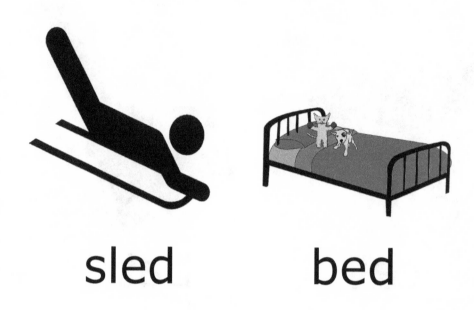

sled   bed

shed   bread

Which is Different?

Can your child pick out the word that doesn't rhyme? Read each word and point to the picture. Tell them three words have the same ending sounds. Ask them to tell you which word does not have the same ending sounds as the other three.

Which of these words do not rhyme?

shoe

two

glue

glove

Which of these words do not rhyme?

sun

hat

bun

one

Which of these words do not rhyme?

car   star

cup   jar

Which are the Same?

Can your child pick out the words that rhyme? Read each word and point to the picture. Tell them three words have the same ending sounds. Ask them to tell you which words have the same ending sounds.

Which of these words rhyme?

seal

wheel

meal

bike

Which of these words rhyme?

plant

tree

bee

key

Which of these words rhyme?

nail

ring

whale

snail

Which Two are the Same?

Can your child pick the word that rhymes with a specific word? Read the top word and point to the picture. Tell them one of the bottom words has the same ending sound and one does not. Point to the bottom pictures as you say each word. Ask them to tell you which words have the same ending sounds.

Which word rhymes with

dog

log   bike

Which word rhymes with

rock

rat

sock

Which word rhymes with

spoon

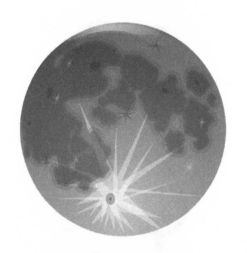

moon

star

Make Your Own Rhyme

Can your child create their own rhyme? Read the word and point to the picture. Ask them to tell you a word that rhymes with the picture. It is okay if they make up their own "silly" word. For example, for cake they could say real words like, "rake, bake, make, snake," or silly words like, "dake, gake, zake," or others.

Tell me a real word or a silly word
that rhymes with

cake

Tell me a real word or a silly word
that rhymes with

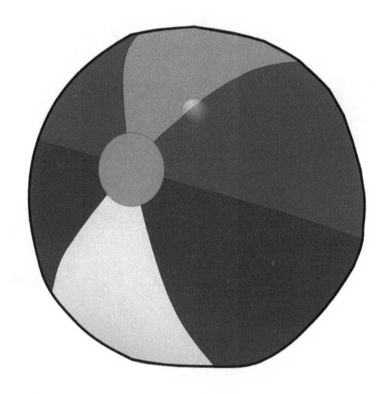

ball

Tell me a real word or a silly word
that rhymes with

cat

If your child needs more help, you can repeat this activity over and over. You can also read rhyming books, sing rhyming songs, make up silly rhymes, especially with your child's name. "Jan ran with Stan the man to buy a fan." Or "Jan, fan, bebop bo ban." You can do this during bath time, while snuggling on the couch, or during any other quiet family time. There are many rhyming activities for free or low cost at:

www.dogonalogbooks.com
www.pinterest.com
www.teacherspayteachers.com

If your child is not mastering rhyming, they can still learn to read. However, the inability to rhyme can be an early symptom of a reading disability. You may wish to contact a trained learning disabilities specialist.

Syllables

Two Words Make One
(Blending Compound Words)

Listen for the clumps of sounds in longer words.

Clap Your Hands

We will start with words that can also be syllables when combined with other words.

Say and clap each word.

cup   cake

Now say and clap the words FAST. Turn the page to see if you got the correct answer.

cupcake

Say and clap each word.

star   fish

Now say and clap the words FAST. Turn the page to see if you got the correct answer.

starfish

Say and clap each word.

horse   shoe

Now say and clap the words FAST. Turn the page to see if you got the correct answer.

horseshoe

Say and clap each word.

sand   box

Now say and clap the words FAST. Turn the page to see if you got the correct answer.

sandbox

Say and clap each word.

skate   board

Now say and clap the words FAST. Turn the page to see if you got the correct answer.

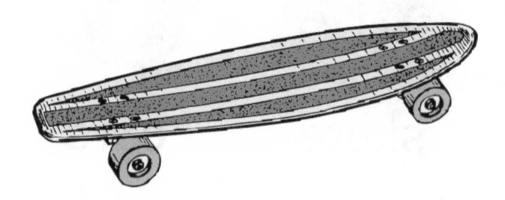

skateboard

If your child needs more help, you can clap the following words then clap them fast to make a new word.

sun*set	back*pack
tea*cup	sail*boat
bath*tub	blue*bird
gold*fish	flag*pole
lunch*box	note*book

You can also play with combining two familiar words to make up a silly two-syllable word.

horse*shirt	dog*couch
lunch*clock	movie*wheel
plant*hat	tree*soup
car*branch	school*sock

Do not progress until your child has mastered this level.

Hear the Syllables
(Segmenting Compound Words)

Listen for the clumps of sounds in the words.

Clap Your Hands

Now it is time to say a word and listen for the syllables.

Say the word and clap each syllable.

cupcake

Turn the page to see if you got the correct answer.

cup cake

Say the word and clap each syllable.

starfish

Turn the page to see if you got the correct answer.

star   fish

Say the word and clap each syllable.

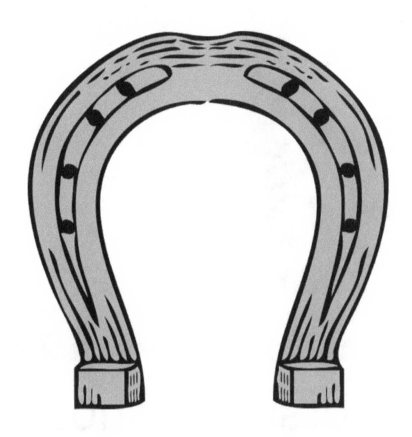

horseshoe

Turn the page to see if you got the correct answer.

horse   shoe

Say the word and clap each syllable.

sandbox

Turn the page to see if you got the correct answer.

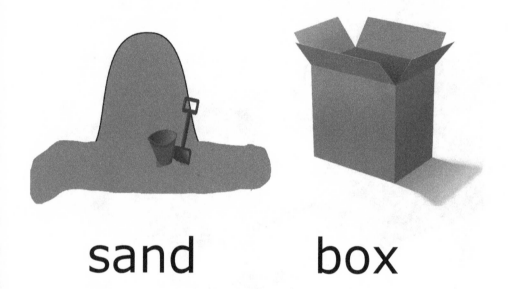

sand   box

Say the word and clap each syllable.

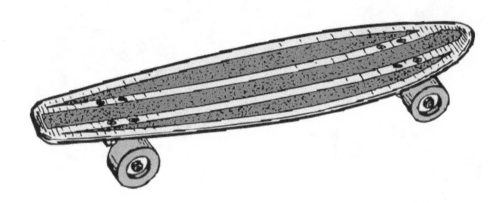

skateboard

Turn the page to see if you got the correct answer.

skate board

If your child needs more help, you can clap the syllables in the following words.

sun*set	back*pack
tea*cup	sail*boat
bath*tub	blue*bird
gold*fish	flag*pole
lunch*box	note*book

You can also play with clapping the syllables in the following silly words and funny words you make up.

horse*shirt	dog*couch
lunch*clock	movie*wheel
plant*hat	tree*soup
car*branch	school*sock

Do not progress until your child has mastered this level. You wouldn't let a teenager drive if they couldn't tell which pedal was the brake and which was the gas.

Funny Syllables
Make Words
(Blending Two-Syllable Words)

Listen for the clumps of sounds in the words.

Clap Your Hands

Now we will learn about syllables that are not words unless they are combined with other syllables.

Say and clap each syllable.

pic   nic

Now say and clap the syllables FAST. Turn the page to see if you got the correct answer.

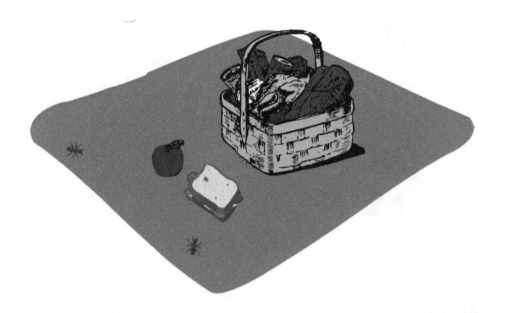

picnic

Say and clap each syllable.

ta   ble

Now say and clap the syllables FAST. Turn the page to see if you got the correct answer.

table

dai   sy

Now say and clap the syllables FAST. Turn the page to see if you got the correct answer.

daisy

Say and clap each syllable.

com   et

Now say and clap the syllables FAST.
Turn the page to see if you got the
correct answer.

comet

Say and clap each syllable.

so   fa

Now say and clap the syllables FAST.
Turn the page to see if you got the
correct answer.

sofa

If your child needs more help, you can clap the following syllables then clap them fast to make a new word.

ep*ic   mim*ic
rel*ish   rad*ish
lim*it   lin*en
un*til   ki*wi

You can also play with combining two syllables to make up a silly two-syllable word.

sup*ic   dit*fob
lun*ish   mot*mun
cas*ric   tren*lom
caf*ren   snef*pon

Do not progress until your child has mastered this level.

Listen for the
Funny Syllables
(Segmenting Two-Syllable Words)

Listen for the clumps of sounds in the words.

Clap Your Hands

Listen to more words and listen for the syllables. If your child can't hear the syllables in the words, have them put their hand under their chin as they say each word. Have them count the number of chin drops. For most words, each time they feel their chin drop it is a syllable. That is because each syllable has a vowel sound and vowel sounds make us open our mouths.

Say the word and clap each syllable.

picnic

Turn the page to see if you got the correct answer.

pic   nic

Say the word and clap each syllable.

table

Turn the page to see if you got the correct answer.

ta   ble

Say the word and clap each syllable.

daisy

Turn the page to see if you got the correct answer.

dai   sy

Say the word and clap each syllable.

comet

Turn the page to see if you got the correct answer.

com   et

Say the word and clap each syllable.

sofa

Turn the page to see if you got the correct answer.

so   fa

If your child needs more help, you can say the following words then clap the syllables.

ep*ic	mim*ic
rel*ish	rad*ish
lim*it	lin*en
un*til	ki*wi

You can also play with saying these silly words and clapping the syllables.

sup*ic	dit*fob
lun*ish	mot*mun
cas*ric	tren*lom
caf*ren	snef*pon

Do not progress until your child has mastered this level.

Longer Words
(Segmenting Three-Syllable Words)

Listen for the clumps of sounds in the words.

Clap Your Hands

Listen to even longer words and clap the syllables.

Say the word and clap each syllable.

elephant

Turn the page to see if you got the correct answer.

el e phant

Say the word and clap each syllable.

parachute

Turn the page to see if you got the correct answer.

par a chute

Say the word and clap each syllable.

mosquito

Turn the page to see if you got the correct answer.

mos qui to

Say the word and clap each syllable.

microwave

Turn the page to see if you got the correct answer.

mi cro wave

Say the word and clap each syllable.

bicycle

Turn the page to see if you got the correct answer.

bi cy cle

If your child needs more help, you can say the following words then clap the syllables.

tel*e*phone   bum*ble*bee
la*dy*bug   dish*wash*er
fin*ger*paint   oct*o*pus

You can also play with saying these silly words and clapping the syllables. What silly words can you and your child create?

trim*sup*ic   bil*dil*fob
flu*lun*ish   trop*mot*mun
pro*cas*tic   tren*lom*ish
cap*caf*ren   scel*pom*et

Take Away a Syllable
(Segmenting Words)

Say the word then take away a syllable
and say the new word.

Clap Your Hands

Listen to the words and clap the syllables. Once your child can clap the syllables, tell them which syllable to take away. Can they state the remaining syllable? Since this is a more difficult activity, the remaining syllable will always be a real word and not a silly syllable.

Remember, we are still working with sounds. Read the syllable sounds to your child. Do not tell them the letters they are supposed to remove.

Say the word and clap each syllable.

popcorn

Now take away "corn."
What do you get?

Turn the page to see if you got the correct answer.

pop

Say the word and clap each syllable.

seahorse

Now take away "sea."
What do you get?

Turn the page to see if you got the correct answer.

horse

Say the word and clap each syllable.

forklift

Now take away "lift."
What do you get?

Turn the page to see if you got the correct answer.

fork

Say the word and clap each syllable.

monkey

Now take away "mon-."
What do you get?

Turn the page to see if you got the correct answer.

key

Say the word and clap each syllable.

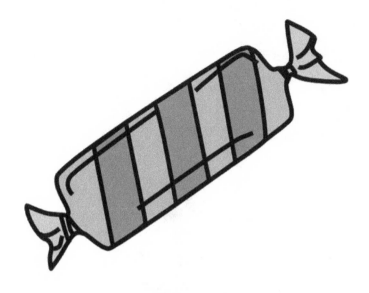

candy

Now take away "-dy."
What do you get?

Turn the page to see if you got the correct answer.

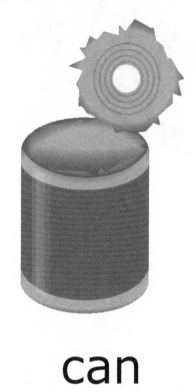

can

Say the word and clap each syllable.

panda

Now take away "-da."
What do you get?

Turn the page to see if you got the correct answer.

pan

You can find more activities for teaching syllables at:

www.dogonalogbooks.com
www.pinterest.com
www.teacherspayteachers.com
www.coxcampus.org

Do not progress until your child has mastered this level.

Tap the Sounds

Before a child can start sounding out words, they need to be able to identify individual sounds in words. The following activities will help your child begin to understand the small sounds within each word. Please continue reading these activities to your child so they can focus on hearing the sounds. Trying to have them sound out the words if they can't identify the individual sounds would likely just be frustrating.

THIS IS IMPORTANT

When making the sounds, be careful to use clear sounds without adding "uh" at the end of the sound. If you say, "B says buh and T says Tuh" then ask your child to read b-a-t, they will probably say, "buh-a-tuh," instead of "bat." You may want to watch a video on how to correctly make each sound. One of my favorite videos for American pronunciations is by Cox Campus/Atlanta Speech School. Here is a direct link to view it on their website:
https://app.coxcampus.org/#!/resourcelibrary/detail/5c38d865706cb4002d363755
You can also find a variety of international videos on YouTube if you search for "44 Phonemes."

TAPPING:
First
sound
in a
word

Tapping is one of the most useful skills a new reader can learn. Once they start sounding out words, they will "tap" a finger to their thumb as they sound out words. It makes it multi-sensory as compared to just saying the sounds. It is also harder to lose track of the letters you are sounding out if you are tapping your fingers for each sound. For the remainder of the activities in this book, have your child tap their thumb to their finger for each sound they identify.

TAPPING:
Second
sound
in a
word

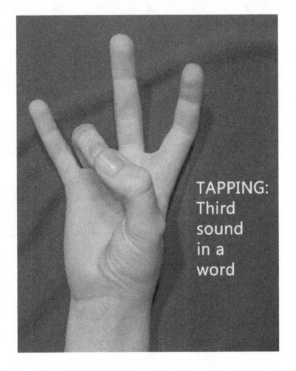

TAPPING:
Third
sound
in a
word

Beginning Sound

Listen for the beginning sound in each word.

Tap your Thumb and Pointer Finger when you say the Beginning Sound

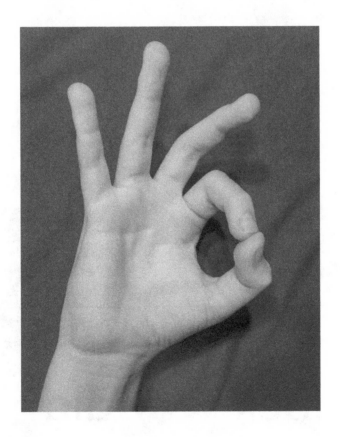

These words have the same beginning sound.

dog

Dad

duck

dig

These words have the same beginning sound.

pig

pan

pop

paw

These words have the same beginning sound.

sun

saw

sis

sock

Do not progress until your child has mastered this level.

Are These the Same?

Now it's time to see if your child can tell which words have the same beginning sound.

Do these words have the same beginning sound?

car

cob

cub

key

Do these words have the same beginning sound?

list

lamb

leaf

log

Do these words have the same beginning sound?

bat   box

bib   bed

Do not progress until your child has mastered this level.

Which is Different?

Can your child pick out the word that does not have the same beginning sound? Read each word and point to the picture. Tell them three words have the same beginning sound. Ask them to tell you which word does not have the same beginning sound as the other three.

Which of these words does not have the same beginning sound?

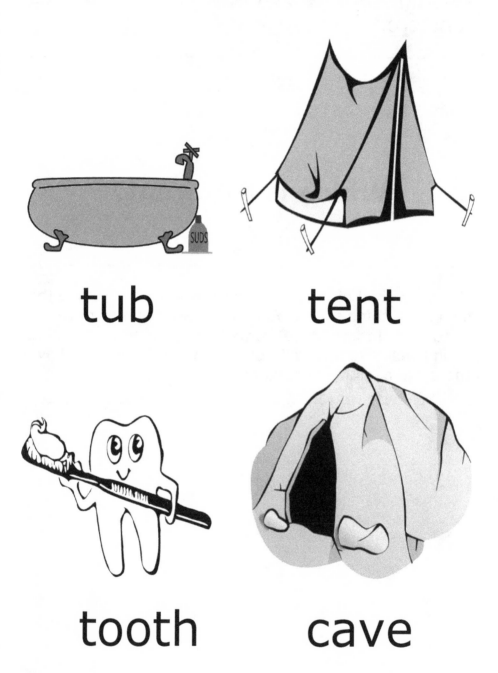

tub   tent

tooth   cave

Which of these words does not have the same beginning sound?

colt

fan

frog

fish

Which of these words does not have the same beginning sound?

jug

jam

jet

leaf

Which are the Same?

Can your child pick out the words that do have the same beginning sound? Read each word and point to the picture. Tell them three words have the same beginning sound. Ask them to tell you which words have the same beginning sound.

Which of these words have the same beginning sound?

lamp   hat

horse   home

Which of these words have the same beginning sound?

plant

pan

bee

pig

Which of these words have the same beginning sound?

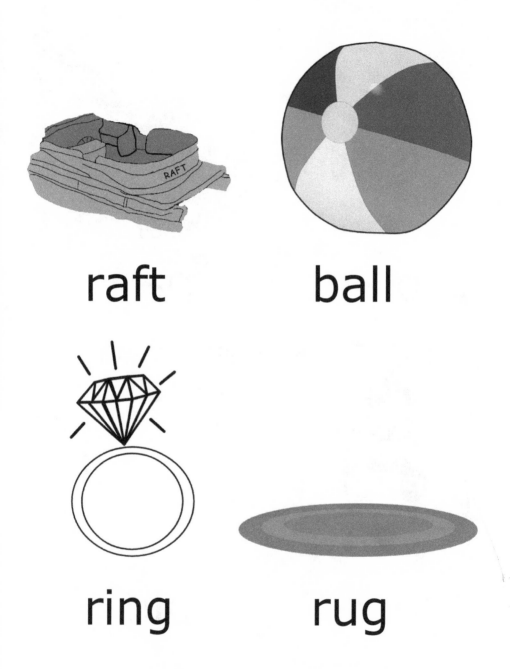

raft

ball

ring

rug

Which Two are the Same?

Can your child pick the word that has the same beginning sound? Read the top word and point to the picture. Tell them one of the bottom words has the same beginning sound and one does not. Point to the bottom pictures as you say each word. Ask them to tell you which words have the same beginning sounds.

Which words have the same beginning sound?

dog

Dad   pan

Which of these words have the same beginning sound?

rock

rat   dig

Which of these words have the same beginning sound?

sun

car   saw

If your child needs more help, you can repeat this activity over and over. You can also read alliteration (same beginning sound) books, sing songs, make up silly sentences, especially with your child's name. "Jan jumps with a jolt just for joy." Or "Jan, joe jan, jeebop joe jan." You can do this during bath time, while snuggling on the couch, or during any other quiet family time. There are many beginning sound activities for free or low cost at:

www.dogonalogbooks.com
www.pinterest.com
www.teacherspayteachers.com
www.coxcampus.org

Do not progress until your child has mastered this level.

Ending Sound

Listen for the ending sound in each word.

These words will all have three sounds so you can
Tap your Thumb and Ring Finger when you say the Ending Sound.

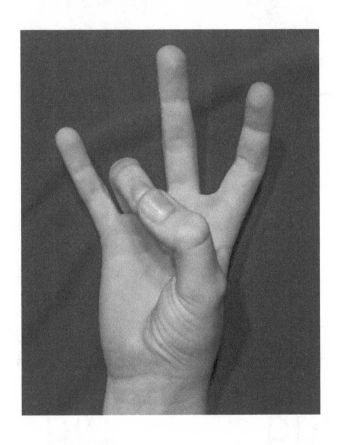

These words have the same ending sound.

dog

bag

rug

pig

These words have the same ending sound.

can

hen

moon

sun

These words have the same ending sound.

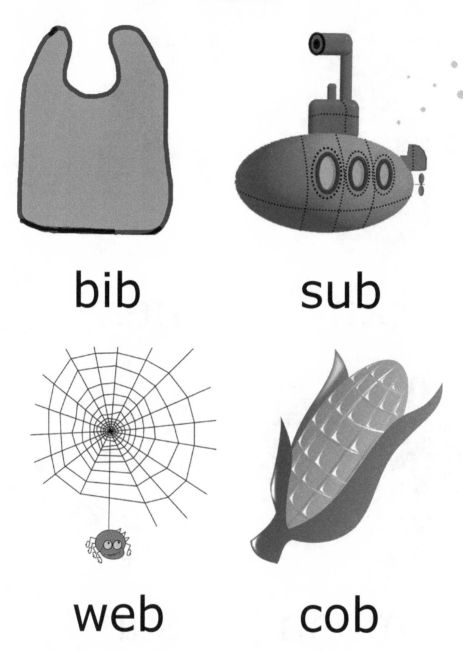

bib   sub

web   cob

> Do not progress until your child has mastered this level.

Are These the Same?

> Now it's time to see if your child can tell which words have the same ending sound.

Do these words have the same ending sound?

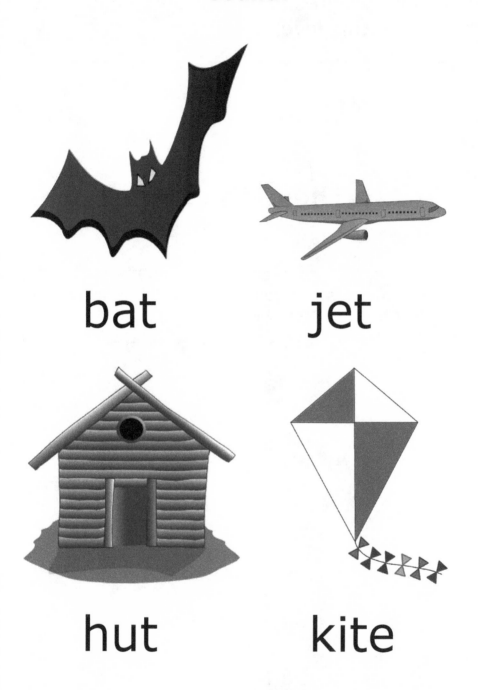

bat

jet

hut

kite

Do these words have the same ending sound?

ship

pup

map

top

Do these words have the same ending sound?

rain

sun

men

can

Do not progress until your child has mastered this level.

Which is Different?

Can your child pick out the word that does not have the same ending sound? Read each word and point to the picture. Tell them three words have the same ending sound. Ask them to tell you which word does not have the same ending sound as the other three.

Which of these words does not have the same ending sound?

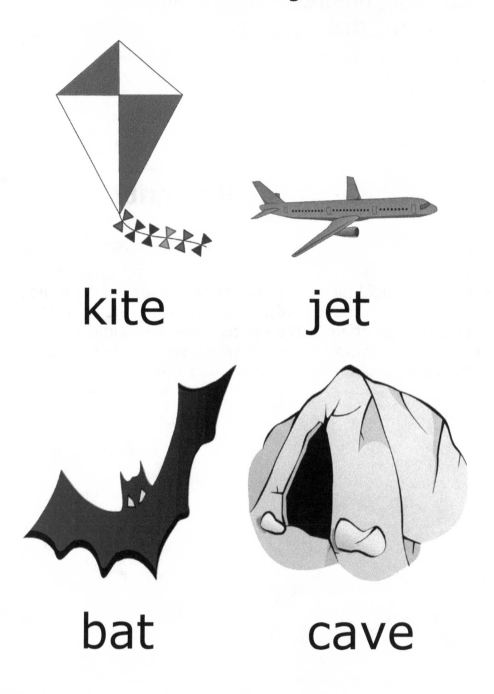

kite

jet

bat

cave

Which of these words does not have the same ending sound?

dig

fan

frog

bug

Which of these words does not have the same ending sound?

pup

top

dog

ship

Which are the Same?

Can your child pick out the words that have the same ending sound? Read each word and point to the picture. Tell them three words have the same ending sound. Ask them to tell you which words have the same ending sound.

Which of these words have the same ending sound?

jet

cat

mop

hut

Which of these words have the same ending sound?

sun   dog

bag   pig

Which of these words have the same ending sound?

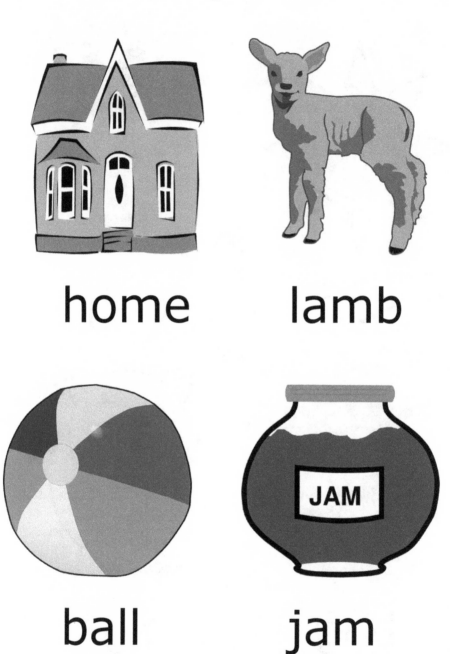

home   lamb

ball   jam

Which Two are the Same?

Can your child pick the word that has the same ending sound? Read the top word and point to the picture. Tell them one of the bottom words has the same ending sound and one does not. Point to the bottom pictures as you say each word. Ask them to tell you which words have the same ending sound.

Which words have the same ending sound?

dog

pig   sun

Which of these words have the same ending sound?

sock

duck

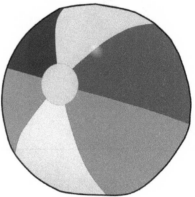

ball

Which of these words have the same ending sound?

sun

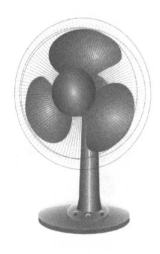

fan

pig

If your child needs more help, you can repeat this activity over and over. You can make up silly sentences, especially with your child's name. Emphasize the ending sound that is the same. "Jan got a sun tan when she ran with Dan in the sun shine." Or "Jan, joe ban, gee-can joe ran." You can do this during bath time, while snuggling on the couch, or during any other quiet family time. There are many ending sounds activities for free or low cost to be found at:

www.dogonalogbooks.com
www.pinterest.com
www.teacherspayteachers.com
www.coxcampus.org

Do not progress until your child has mastered this level.

Middle Sound

Listen for the middle sound in each word.

These words will all have three sounds so you can

Tap your Thumb and Middle Finger when you say the Middle Sound

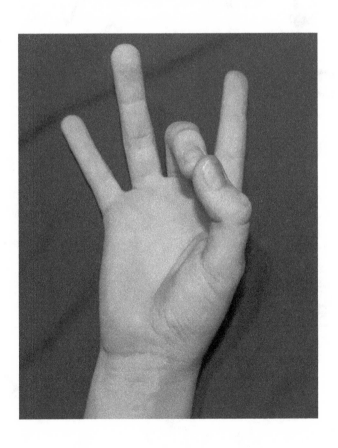

These words have the same middle sound.

pup

sun

hut

duck

These words have the same middle sound.

can   lamb

bat   Dad

These words have the same middle sound.

bib

pig

fish

sis

Do not progress until your child has mastered this level.

Are These the Same?

Now it's time to see if your child can tell which words have the same middle sound.

Do these words have the same middle sound?

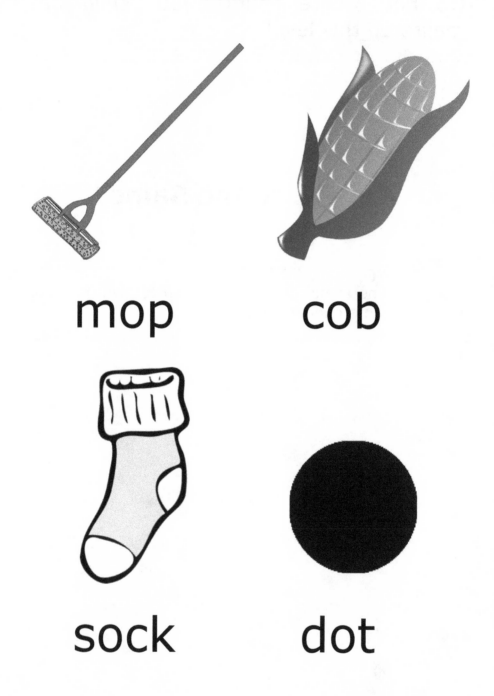

mop   cob

sock   dot

Do these words have the same middle sound?

bed

men

net

wreck

Do these words have the same middle sound?

pan

lamb

cat

Dad

Which is Different?

Can your child pick out the word that does not have the same middle sound? Read each word and point to the picture. Tell them three words have the same middle sound. Ask them to tell you which word does not have the same middle sound as the other three.

Which of these words does not have the same middle sound?

bat

ram

pan

dig

Which of these words does not have the same middle sound?

dig

sis

fish

hat

Which of these words does not have the same middle sound?

pup

sun

dog

hut

Which are the Same?

Can your child pick out the words that have the same middle sound? Read each word and point to the picture. Tell them three words have the same middle sound. Ask them to tell you which words have the same middle sound.

Which of these words have the same middle sound?

jet

bed

men

hut

Which of these words have the same middle sound?

fish

hut

bug

sun

Which of these words have the same middle sound?

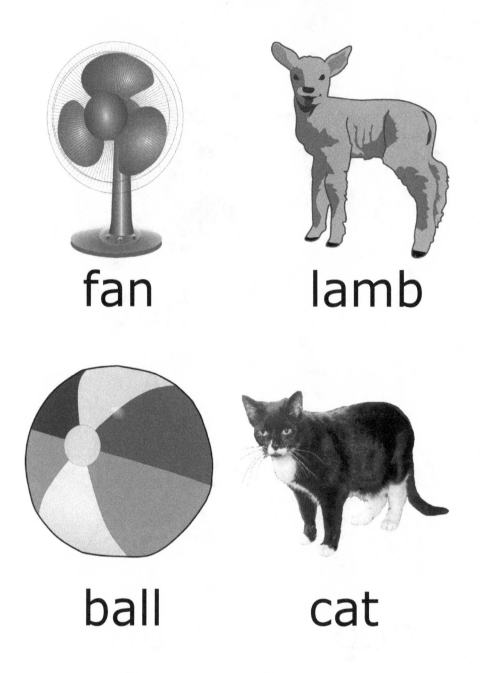

fan   lamb

ball   cat

Which Two are the Same?

Can your child pick the word that has the same middle sound? Read the top word and point to the picture. Tell them one of the bottom words has the same middle sound and one does not. Point to the bottom pictures as you say each word. Ask them to tell you which words have the same middle sound.

Which words have the same middle sound?

pup

fish   sun

Which of these words have the same middle sound?

sock

mop

dig

Which of these words have the same middle sound?

sun

bug

hat

If your child needs more help, you can repeat this activity over and over. Finding fun word games may be harder than with beginning sounds. You can make up silly sentences, especially with your child's name. Emphasize the middle sound that is the same. "J**a**n h**a**s a l**a**mb with a h**a**t th**a**t r**a**n to the d**a**m." You can do this during bath time, while snuggling on the couch, or any other quiet family time. There are many middle sound activities for free or at low cost at:

www.dogonalogbooks.com
www.pinterest.com
www.teacherspayteachers.com
www.coxcampus.org

Blending Sounds

Listen to the words. Add a new sound to create a new word.

These words will all have two or three sounds so you can tap them to help your child practice tapping sounds. This will help them a lot when it is time to start reading.

Read the words. Once your child can say the word, read them the sound they must add to make a new word.

Remember, we are still working with sounds. Read the words and sounds to your child. Do not tell them the letters they are adding. When you see a letter in brackets like this /a/ you pronounce the sound of that letter.

Say this word:

an

Now add the sound /p/ at the beginning.

What new word did you get?

You should have gotten:

pan

Say this word:

an

Now add the sound /m/ at the beginning.

What new word did you get?

You should have gotten:

man

Say this word:

am

Now add the sound /j/ at the beginning.

What new word did you get?

You should have gotten:

jam

Say this word:

am

Now add the sound /d/ at the beginning.

What new word did you get?

You should have gotten:

dam

Say this silly word:

ag

Now add the sound /d/ at the beginning.

What new silly word did you get?

You should have gotten:

dag

Say this word:

too

Now add the sound /t/ at the ending.

What new word did you get?

You should have gotten:

toot

Say this word:

so

Now add the sound /p/ at the ending.

What new word did you get?

You should have gotten:

soap

Say this word:

be

Now add the sound /p/ at the ending.

What new word did you get?

You should have gotten:

beep

Say this silly word:

zi

Now add the sound /m/ at the ending.

What new silly word did you get?

You should have gotten:

zim

If your child needs more help, you can repeat this activity over and over. You can add letter sounds to the beginning or end of short words to make more real words or silly words. For example, to the word "an" you can add beginning sounds /b/ /d/ /f/ /j/ /r/ /t/ /v./ This will make words such as "Dan" and "fan." For ending sounds, you can add sounds to the word "be." /d/ /f/ /k/ /m/ /p/ /t./ This will make words such as "bead" and "beak."

Do not progress until your child has mastered this level.

Removing Sounds
(Segmenting)

Listen to the words. Remove a sound to create a new word.

These words will all have two or three sounds so you can tap them to help your child practice tapping sounds. This will help them a lot when it is time to start reading.

Read the words. Once your child can say the word, read them the sound they must remove to make a new word.

Remember, we are still working with sounds. Read the words and sounds to your child. Do not tell them the letters they are removing. When you see a letter in brackets like this /a/ you pronounce the sound of that letter.

Say this word:

cat

Now take away the sound /c/

What new word did you get?

You should have gotten:

at

Say this word:

pat

Now take away the sound /p/

What new word did you get?

You should have gotten:

at

Say this word:

fit

Now take away the sound /f/

What new word did you get?

You should have gotten:

it

Say this word:

lit

Now take away the sound /l/

What new word did you get?

You should have gotten:

it

Say this silly word:

hib

Now take away the sound /h/

What new silly word did you get?

You should have gotten:

ib

Say this word:

beet

Now take away the sound /t/

What new word did you get?

You should have gotten:

be

Say this word:

soak

Now take away the sound /k/

What new word did you get?

You should have gotten:

so

Say this silly word:

fime

Now take away the sound /m/

What new silly word did you get?

You should have gotten:

fie

If your child needs more help, you can repeat this activity over and over. You can add or remove sounds to or from the beginning or end of short words to make more real words or silly words.

Do not progress until your child has mastered all these skills. If your child cannot distinguish the sounds in words, it is unlikely they will be able to sound out words.

If your child has mastered all the sounds in this book, it is time to start learning the sounds of the letters and learning how to blend them into words. The next book in this series, *The Squiggle Code (Letters Make Words)* will help them learn to do this.

STRUGGLING READERS

Excerpts from
Teaching a Struggling Reader:
One Mom's Experience with Dyslexia

What if it's NOT Dyslexia

The Importance of Early Intervention

(Links to the online resources are provided as endnotes.)

What If It's NOT Dyslexia

Sixty-five percent of fourth graders in the US are <u>not proficient at reading</u>.[i] Most of these children do not have dyslexia. I have spoken with numerous education professionals and read many articles including this one on <u>APM Reports</u>.[ii] The reason these children are not proficient with reading is usually because they are not taught reading with phonics. Their teachers were usually not taught how to teach phonics even though scientific research shows that systematic phonics is the best way for any student to learn to read.

The National Reading Panel reviewed 100,000 studies that examined reading instruction. They stated, "Systematic and explicit phonics instruction is more effective than non-systematic or no phonics instruction." In other words, the best way to learn to read is to be taught with a systematic phonics program. You can read their booklet <u>here</u>.[iii]

If your child is a struggling reader who has been taught with Whole Language or Balanced Literacy, you may want to approach their teacher, principal, or school board and asked them to review the scientific literature that says your child should be taught systematic explicit phonics. Then insist they teach all their students phonics in a scientifically proven manner. You may also consider using a program like <u>All About Reading</u>,[iv] <u>Explode the Code</u>,[v] or <u>MindPlay Virtual Reading Program</u>[vi] to teach them phonics yourself. Dr. Nancy Mather, a professor at the University of Arizona, has been very helpful to me and my books. You may want to check out the phonics program she co-authored: <u>Phonic Reading Lessons: Skills and Practice</u>.[vii]

My book, *The Squiggle Code (Letters Make Words,)* is a roadmap for teaching letter sounds, blending, and the beginning steps of reading. It is priced to be economical and there are numerous printable activities you can download from www.dogonalogbooks.com/printables that will supplement the material in the book.

A PBS partner, Education Week, produced this video, Parents of Students With Dyslexia Have Transformed Reading Instruction.[viii] It talks about how the advocacy of parents with children who have dyslexia has changed how all children in Arkansas are taught to read.

Here is basic information and an outline on the teaching of reading:

When teaching letter sounds, many parents and teachers demonstrate incorrect sounds. They may say, "B says buh and T says Tuh." Then they ask the child to read b-a-t. The child will say, "buh-a-tuh," instead of "bat." This 44 Phonemes video[ix] will show you the correct way to make each of the 44 sounds in the (American) English language.

Although there can be more to it, the process of teaching reading with phonics is basically:

• Work on segmenting and blending.[x] There are many resources on Pinterest.[xi]

• Start by teaching the sounds of a few letters in a multisensory way. Draw them in shaving cream, trace them with your fingers, or any other fun way.

• After your student(s) have learned those letter sounds, sound out a few words with the letters they've been taught so far. Have your child put a finger under each letter and say the sounds as fast as they can until the child can say the whole word.

• Teach a few more letters.

- Sound out more words with those letters.

- Teach sight words, a few at a time. <u>Dolch words</u>[xii] are common sight words.

- Have the child read short decodable texts that provide practice with these letters and sounds.
- Move on to more individual phonics rules. Find a systematic decodable reading program. When they have mastered a set of phonics rules, move on to the next set of rules.

- Teach them about the six syllable types and how they may help determine the vowel sounds in words.

- Make sure to incorporate writing and reading the learned sounds/rules/sight words at each step of the way. Don't just focus on the rules, they need to practice reading and writing.

- My personal recommendation is to teach any learning reader to "tap" while sounding out. (See the earlier section on "tapping.") Some children may to try to guess at a word, but if they are tapping it really focuses them on the letters on the page so they will actually read it.

Here is a recommended order of teaching individual letter sounds. It is from *Phonic Reading Lessons* by Nancy Mather Ph.D., et al., 2007.

1. Vowel a: consonants s, m, f, t, n
2. No new vowel: consonants r, d, c, g
3. Vowel o; no new consonants
4. No new vowel; consonants b, h, l x
5. Vowel i; consonants p, k, j
6. Review of a, o, i, and 16 consonants
7. Vowel u; consonants y, z qu
8. Vowel e; consonants v, w
9. Review of u, e

The Importance of Early Intervention

The importance of early intervention cannot be stressed enough. Many teachers will tell parents, "Your child is just a late bloomer. They'll get it when they're ready. Let's just wait and watch." Although it is true that kids learn in different ways and at different rates, it seems individuals with dyslexia are pretty much born with different brains. The earlier they receive intervention, the better they may become at reading. <u>Tackling Dyslexia at an Early Age</u>[xiii] from Harvard Medical school states, "up to 70 percent of at-risk children who receive educational intervention in kindergarten or first grade become proficient readers." This article also talks about changes that occur in the brain with early school-age interventions.

On January 27, 2005, <u>Reading Rockets did an online chat with Dr. Sally Shaywitz</u>,[xiv] Dr, Shaywitz *(co-director of the <u>Yale Center for Dyslexia and Creativity</u>,[xv] at Yale University)* gave this list of signs seen in preschool children with dyslexia. If find it so important that I am including it in its entirety:

The most important clues in a preschool child are:

- *A family history of reading problems*
- *Delayed speech*
- *Lack of appreciation and enjoyment of rhymes e.g., not appreciating the rhymes in a Dr. Seuss book*
- *Not being able to recite rhymes by age 3*
- *Continuation of baby talk*
- *Trouble pronouncing words*
- *Trouble learning the alphabet (not the alphabet song, but knowing the individual names of the letters of the alphabet)*

It is important to keep in mind that you are looking for a pattern of these clues, ones that keeping occurring often. Not knowing a rhyme or the name of a letter once or twice is not what we are looking for. A pattern that occurs over and over again is what to look for.

A parent may be concerned their child could have dyslexia because of <u>red flags in their child's behavior</u>[xvi] or because of <u>family history</u>.[xvii] It seems to me that if a parent is concerned their child younger than 5 may have dyslexia, that taking actions at that early age could be highly beneficial. I have done multiple searches and contacted many dyslexia professionals asking for specific interventions to help preschool children who may have dyslexia. My online searches found no specific recommendations for how to help preschool children who may have dyslexia. Fortunately, I did receive very helpful information from two well-regarded Dyslexia Professionals.

Joanne Marttila Pierson, Ph.D., CCC-SLP, the Project Manager of <u>DyslexiaHelp</u>[xviii] at the University of Michigan stated, "Your best bet is to write about spoken language skills and development. As you know, spoken language undergirds learning to read, spell, and write, and so the better linguistic skills a child has, the better he is likely to do learning to read. For example, I have a <u>developmental milestone checker here</u>.[xix] As is suggested in this article, <u>Is Preschool Language Impairment a Risk Factor for Dyslexia in Adolescence?</u>,[xx] children with phonological disorders in preschool are at greater risk for reading disorder, which makes sense since the core deficit in dyslexia is in phonological processing (i.e., phonological awareness, phonological memory, rapid automatic naming.) And, books such as *Beyond Bedtime Stories* by Nell Duke are what you'd want to offer as resources."

As Dr. Pierson stated, many children with dyslexia have speech delays. Receiving Speech Therapy from a Speech Pathologist could make a tremendous difference when they start learning to read. (It will also be useful even if they do not have dyslexia.) When both of my children were babies, I frequently used the <u>Ages and Stages Questionnaires</u>^{xxi} just to make sure they were developing on target. When the results showed my daughter's speech was behind schedule, I got her evaluated. Because of this my daughter was able to start Speech Therapy at twelve months of age.

I'd always thought Speech Therapy was teaching children how to say words. Actually, articulation has been a very minor part of her therapy. It has focused more on helping her understand and express words. Speech Therapy helps children say, "I want the firetruck book." instead of "I want that." Early Intervention services are often free or very low cost for children from birth to three. Many school districts will continue with the (often free) services once the child turns three. You can learn more about <u>Early Intervention here</u>.^{xxii}

Reading to young children is perhaps one of the most important activities you can share. We read to our children multiple times a day during the early years. My daughter wanted to be read to even more than my son. She couldn't talk so she would scream if I didn't read to her for hours every day. I had the luxury of being a Stay-At-Home-Mom so we sat together reading book after book after book every day. I am not exaggerating when I say we read for hours each day for months, possibly years (those years are such a blur that I don't remember how long they lasted.) I now wonder if she craved being read to so much because she could not understand what language was and if being read to helped her try to figure it out. This article discusses <u>10 Benefits That Highlight the Importance of Reading with Young Children</u>.^{xxiii}

Another Dyslexia professional, Susan Barton of <u>Bright Solutions for Dyslexia</u>,[xxiv] also contacted me. She stated, "Most dyslexia professionals will not screen or test a child younger than age 5 1/2, plus the child must be at least halfway through kindergarten. But if you suspect dyslexia, I recommend you start doing the activities described in the following books now."

- *Phonemic Awareness in Young Children: A Classroom Curriculum* by Marilyn Adams Ph.D. and Barbara Foorman "Ph.D. M.A.T"

- *Preparing Children for Success in Reading: A Multisensory Guide for Teachers and Parents* by Nancy Sanders Royal based on the work of Beth Slingerland.

Since I could find no online links to share that explicitly said how to help preschool children who may have dyslexia, I searched for ways of teaching phonemic awareness in early childhood. Reading Rockets has a <u>list of specific activities</u>[xxv] that promote phonemic awareness. My favorite dyslexia website, <u>Homeschooling With Dyslexia</u>,[xxvi] has good phonemic awareness ideas. Pinterest is a great source for Phonemic Awareness. This link to <u>Pinterest</u>[xxvii] will offer you scads of ideas. I also searched for activities that would help any child gain skills to improve their reading abilities. There is an excellent list of suggestions at this article, <u>Help for Young Readers</u>.[xxviii]

As a parent, it can be really overwhelming to find and figure out exactly what skills are involved in phonological and phonemic awareness. As I was researching this, my eyes would sometimes roll back in my head from all the didactic information I found. Paragraph after paragraph of theory and information that was just so boring to read and didn't often tell me what activities were useful. I figured if I was overwhelmed trying to figure it all out, other parents might be at least as overwhelmed and frustrated. (I have the good fortune to have several dyslexia/reading/phonics experts that answer my questions, but many parents don't have that.)

This is why I have created this set of DOG ON A LOG Pup Books. I made them a Parent-Friendly Roadmap that show which skills kids need to learn and in which order. Because it is important that activities are personalized for each child, I include resources for where other activities can be found for free or low-cost. To make the search simpler for families, I have created boardgames and other activities that can be downloaded from my website.[xxix] There are activities for each section of The Squiggle Code Books. You do not need to read the books to use the activities. If you use the printable activities in order, you will be working on all the phonological and phonemic awareness skills.

My daughter and I have played the boardgames as a way to practice her sight words. In the homeschool co-op phonics class I taught, we played the same boardgames to practice rhyming, beginning/ending/middle sounds, and so much more. The boardgames can be adapted to any child's needs simply by switching out the game cards.

Please note. Although playing games and doing activities such as making up fun rhymes, counting syllables, and changing some of the sounds in words can be fun and advantageous for preschool children, I am not advocating teaching very young children to read. Children should not be forced to read before they are developmentally ready. One of my favorite books *Einstein Never Used Flashcards: How Our Children Really Learn-- And Why They Need to Play More and Memorize Less* by Kathy Hirsh-Pasek discusses multiple studies that show that children in play-based preschools ultimately do better than children in academic-based preschools. This pdf[xxx] also discusses the potential downsides of introducing reading at too young of an age.

Writing this section on Early Intervention brought out some of my Mom-Guilt. The *Help for Young Readers* article suggests rhyming activities with young children. We did lots of that with our son when he was a toddler and preschooler. It was so much fun. Then we tried it with our daughter. It wasn't so much fun. She didn't get it. No matter how many playful rhymes we made with her name or what we were saying and no matter how many rhyming books we read, she never understood rhyming. We eventually stopped trying. (She would learn to rhyme after multiple sessions with two different Orton-Gillingham teachers.) My guilty side wonders if we had kept trying to teach her rhyming and had done more phonemic awareness activities if it would have helped her when it was time to learn to read. We didn't know rhyming challenges could be a sign of dyslexia so we just stopped doing it and moved on to other ways to have fun with her.

We did so many good things for our daughter (we still do,) but I so regret we didn't do more phonemic awareness activities. I say this because, now that I know what activities we could have done, I think how hard parenting can be. For Stay-Home parents, not getting a break tires you out so much. For working parents there just aren't enough hours in a day. Every parent wants to do what is best for their child and sometimes (or often) life gets in the way. Please know that if you're feeling guilty that you can't do it all, you're not the only one that feels that way. Also know that every little action you take will make a difference in the long run. My husband likes to say, "Wrigley Gum made their fortune selling 5 cent packs of gum." (Ironically, William Wrigley Jr. of the chewing gum company had dyslexia.) Our daughter benefited from every book we read her and every Speech Therapy session she attended, even the ones where she refused to cooperate for half the session.

How You Can Help

Parents often worry that their child (or even adult learner) is not going to learn to read. Hearing other people's successes (especially when they struggled) can give worried parents or teachers hope. I would encourage others to share their experiences with products you've used by posting reviews at your favorite bookseller(s) stating how your child benefitted from those books or materials (whether it was DOG ON A LOG Books or another book or product.) This will help other parents and teachers know which products they should consider using. More than that, hearing your successes could truly help another family feel hopeful. It's amazing that something as seemingly small as a review can ease someone's concerns.

Phonics Progression

DOG ON A LOG Pup Books

Book 1

Phonological/Phonemic Awareness:
- Words
- Rhyming
- Syllables, identification, blending, segmenting
- Identifying individual letter sounds

Books 2-3

Phonemic Awareness/Phonics
- Consonants, primary sounds
- Short vowels
- Blending
- Introduction to sight words

DOG ON A LOG Let's GO! and Chapter Books

Step 1
- Consonants, primary sounds
- Short vowels
- Digraphs: ch, sh, th, wh, ck
- 2 and 3 sound words
- Possessive 's
-

Step 2
- Bonus letters (f, l, s, z after short vowel)
- "all"
- –s suffix

Step 3
- Letter Buddies: ang, ing, ong, ung, ank, ink, onk, unk

Step 4
- Consonant blends to make 4 sound words
- 3 and 4 sound words ending in –lk, -sk

Step 5
- Digraph blend –nch to make 3 and 4 sound words
- Silent e, including "-ke"

Step 6
- Exception words containing: ild, old, olt, ind, ost

Step 7
- 5 sounds in a closed syllable word plus suffix -s (crunch, slumps)
- 3 letter blends and up to 6 sounds in a closed syllable word (script, spring)

Step 8
- Two-syllable words with 2 closed syllables, not blends (sunset, chicken, unlock)

Step 9
- Two-syllable words with all previously introduced sounds including blends, exception words, and silent "e" (blacksmith, kindness, inside)
- Vowel digraphs: ai, ay, ea, ee, ie, oa, oe (rain, play, beach, tree, pie, boat, toe)

WATCH FOR MORE STEPS COMING SOON

DOG ON A LOG Books
Sight Word Progression

DOG ON A LOG Pup Books
a, does, go, has, her is, of, says, the, to

DOG ON A LOG Let's GO! and
Chapter Books

Step 1
a, and, are, be, does, go, goes, has, he, her, his, into, is, like, my, of, OK, says, see, she, the, they, to, want, you

Step 2
could, do, eggs, for, from, have, here, I, likes, me, nest, onto, or, puts, said, say, sees, should, wants, was, we, what, would, your

Step 3
as, Mr., Mrs., no, put, their, there, where

Step 4
push, saw

Step 5
come, comes, egg, pull, pulls, talk, walk, walks

Step 6
Ms., so, some, talks

Step 7
Hmmm, our, out, Pop E., TV

Step 8
Dr., friend, full, hi, island, people, please

Step 9
about, aunt, cousin, cousins, down, friends, hi, inn, know, knows, me, one, ones, TVs, two, water, welcome

More DOG ON A LOG Books

Most books available in Paperback, Hardback, and e-book formats

DOG ON A LOG Parent and Teacher Guides

Book 1 (Also in FREE e-book and PDF Bookfold)
- Teaching a Struggling Reader: One Mom's Experience with Dyslexia

Book 2 (FREE e-book and PDF Bookfold only)
- How to Use Decodable Books to Teach Reading

DOG ON A LOG Pup Books
Book 1
- Before the Squiggle Code (A Roadmap to Reading)

Books 2-3
- The Squiggle Code (Letters Make Words)
- Kids' Squiggles (Letters Make Words)

Let's GO! Books have less text

Chapter Books are longer

DOG ON A LOG Let's GO! and Chapter Books

Step 1
- The Dog on the Log
- The Pig Hat
- Chad the Cat
- Zip the Bug
- The Fish and the Pig

Step 2
- Mud on the Path
- The Red Hen
- The Hat and Bug Shop
- Babs the 'Bot
- The Cub

Step 3
- Mr. Bing has Hen Dots
- The Junk Lot Cat
- Bonk Punk Hot Rod
- The Ship with Wings
- The Sub in the Fish Tank

Step 4
- The Push Truck
- The Sand Hill
- Lil Tilt and Mr. Ling
- Musk Ox in the Tub
- The Trip to the Pond

Step 5
- Bake a Cake
- The Crane at the Cave
- Ride a Bike
- Crane or Crane?
- The Swing Gate

Step 6

- The Colt
- The Gold Bolt
- Hide in the Blinds
- The Stone Child
- Tolt the Kind Cat

Step 7

- Quest for A Grump Grunt
- The Blimp
- The Spring in the Lane
- Stamp for a Note
- Stripes and Splats

Step 8

- Anvil and Magnet
- The Mascot
- Kevin's Rabbit Hole
- The Humbug Vet and Medic Shop
- Chickens in the Attic

Step 9

- Trip to Cactus Gulch 1: The Step-Up Team
- Trip to Cactus Gulch 2: Into the Mineshaft
- Play the Bagpipes
- The Hidden Tale 1: The Lost Snapshot

All chapter books can be purchased individually or with all the same-step books in one volume.

Steps 1-5 can be bought as Let's GO! Books which are less text companions to the chapter books.

All titles can be bought as chapter books.

WATCH FOR MORE BOOKS COMING SOON

DOG ON A LOG
Quick Assessment

Have your child read the following words. If they can't read every word in a Step, that is probably where in the series they should start. Some children may benefit starting at an earlier step to help them build confidence in their reading abilities.

Get a printable assessment sheet at:
www.dogonalogbooks.com/how-to-use/
assessment-tool/

Step 1
fin, mash, sock, sub, cat, that, Dan's

Step 2
less, bats, tell, mall, chips, whiff, falls

Step 3
bangs, dank, honk, pings, chunk, sink, gong, rungs

Step 4
silk, fluff, smash, krill, drop, slim, whisk

Step 5
hunch, crate, rake, tote, inch, mote, lime

Step 6
child, molts, fold, hind, jolt, post, colds

Step 7
strive, scrape, splint, twists, crunch, prints, blend

Step 8
finish, denim, within, bathtub, sunset, medic, habit

Step 9
hundred, goldfinch, free, wheat, inhale, play, Joe

Step 10
be, remake, spry, repeat, silo, sometime, pinwheel

WATCH FOR MORE STEPS COMING SOON

Endnotes for Hyperlinks

What if it's NOT Dyslexia

i
https://www.nationsreportcard.gov/reading_math_2015/#reading?grade=4

ii https://www.apmreports.org/story/2018/09/10/hard-words-why-american-kids-arent-being-taught-to-read

iii https://lincs.ed.gov/publications/pdf/PRFbooklet.pdf

iv
https://www.allaboutlearningpress.net/go.php?id=1605&url=4520
v https://www.explodethecode.com/

vi https://mindplay.com/

vii
https://www.highnoonbooks.com/detailHNB.tpl?eqskudatarq=FP8446-X

viii https://www.youtube.com/watch?v=J6fyNvtp1r8

ix
https://www.youtube.com/watch?v=wBuA589kfMg&fbclid=IwAR0hs62XqzvfdwTziEMJA8A5Uhs6fQ6ZGL3KljBUrTIMS1UuwAdJ-0UujTE

x http://www.allkindsofminds.org/word-decoding-blending-and-segmenting-sounds-impact-of-memory

xi
https://www.pinterest.com/search/pins/?q=phonics%20segmenting%20blending&rs=typed&term_meta%5B%5D=phonics|typed&term_meta%5B%5D=segmenting|typed&term_meta%5B%5D=blending|typed

xii https://sightwords.com/sight-words/dolch/

The Importance of Early Intervention

xiii
https://hms.harvard.edu/sites/default/files/publications%20archive/OnTheBrain/OnTheBrainFall14.pdf?fbclid=IwAR3FdX8UNRs7qh6KI_0K03zzFKaSGoc9sLbR5PM5EdBqUCI6ZGWckEkOV6U

xiv https://www.readingrockets.org/article/online-chat-dr-sally-shaywitz

xv http://dyslexia.yale.edu/the-center/our-mission/

xvi https://kidshealth.org/en/parents/dyslexia.html

xvii https://www.dyslexia.com/question/inheritance-of-dyslexia/

xviii http://dyslexiahelp.umich.edu/

xix http://dyslexiahelp.umich.edu/parents/learn-about-dyslexia/is-my-child-dyslexic/developmental-milestones/birth-6-years

xx https://www.cambridge.org/core/journals/journal-of-child-psychology-and-psychiatry-and-allied-disciplines/article/is-preschool-language-impairment-a-risk-factor-for-dyslexia-in-adolescence/793440F296AE989B6430457054D34F4E

xxi https://agesandstagesresearch.com/en

xxii

https://www.google.com/search?q=understood+org+earl
y+intervention+and+what+it+is&oq=understood+org+e
arly+intervention+and+what+it+is&aqs=chrome..69i57.
10423j1j7&sourceid=chrome&ie=UTF-8

xxiii https://bilingualkidspot.com/2017/10/19/benefits-
importance-reading-young-children/

xxiv https://www.dys-add.com/

xxv http://www.readingrockets.org/article/phonemic-
activities-preschool-or-elementary-classroom

xxvi https://homeschoolingwithdyslexia.com/teach-
phonemic-awareness-kids-dyslexia/ref/70/

xxvii

https://www.pinterest.com/search/pins/?rs=ac&len=2&q
=phonemic%20awareness%20activities%20preschool&e
q=phonemic%20awareness&etslf=8718&term_meta%5B
%5D=phonemic|autocomplete|3&term_meta%5B%5D=a
wareness|autocomplete|3&term_meta%5B%5D=activitie
s|autocomplete|3&term_meta%5B%5D=preschool|autoc
omplete|3

xxviii https://www.smartkidswithld.org/getting-
help/dyslexia/help-young-readers/

xxix https://dogonalogbooks.com/printables/

xxx

https://www.deyproject.org/uploads/1/5/5/7/15571834/r
eadinginkindergarten_online-1__1_.pdf

CPSIA information can be obtained
at www.ICGtesting.com
Printed in the USA
LVHW111330020622
720240LV00003B/19